THE PORTABLE CRAFTER
KNITTING

THE PORTABLE CRAFTER
KNITTING

Leanne Bennett

Sterling Publishing Co., Inc.
New York
A Sterling/Chapelle Book

Chapelle, Ltd.

Jo Packham • Sara Toliver • Cindy Stoeckl

Editor: Leslie Farmer
Photography: Kevin Dilley for Hazen Photography
Photo Stylist: Suzy Skadburg
Art Director: Karla Haberstich
Copy Editor: Marilyn Goff
Staff: Kelly Ashkettle, Areta Bingham, Anne Bruns, Donna Chambers,
       Ray Cornia, Emily Frandsen, Lana Hall, Susan Jorgensen,
       Jennifer Luman, Melissa Maynard, Barbara Milburn,
       Lecia Monsen, Kim Taylor, Linda Venditti, Desirée Wybrow

Library of Congress Cataloging-in-Publication Data

Bennett, Leanne.
The portable crafter. Knitting / Leanne Bennett.
  p. cm.
"A Sterling/Chapelle Book."
Includes index.
ISBN 1-4027-0934-X
1. Knitting--Patterns. I. Title: Knitting. II. Title. III. Portable crafter.
TT825.B39 2004
746.43'20432--dc22

              2003027782

10 9 8 7 6 5 4 3 2 1

Published by Sterling Publishing Co., Inc.
387 Park Avenue South, New York, NY 10016
©2004 by Leanne Bennett
Distributed in Canada by Sterling Publishing
c/o Canadian Manda Group, One Atlantic Avenue, Suite 105
Toronto, Ontario, Canada M6K 3E7
Distributed in Great Britain by Chrysalis Books Group PLC,
The Chrysalis Building, Bramley Road, London W10 6SP, England
Distributed in Australia by Capricorn Link (Australia) Pty. Ltd.
P.O. Box 704, Windsor, NSW 2756, Australia
Printed in China
All Rights Reserved

Sterling ISBN 1-4027-0934-X

If you have questions or comments, please contact:

Chapelle, Ltd., Inc.,
P.O. Box 9252, Ogden, UT 84409
(801) 621-2777 • (801) 621-2788 Fax
e-mail: chapelle@chapelleltd.com
web site: chapelleltd.com

TABLE OF CONTENTS

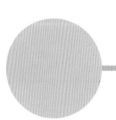

INTRODUCTION

The art of knitting began approximately 3,000 years ago in Arabia. Men of Nomadic tribes would use the wool from their goats and sheep. The women of the tribe would gather and spin, but were not allowed to knit. The first "on the go" knitting was introduced by the Arabian traders who took their art on their travels and taught their techniques to people they would meet in various ports.

The Golden Age of knitting was around the 200-year period between the late 1400s and the 1600s. Knitting guilds all over Europe were founded to maintain the high standards of excellence of the craft. Master knitting was a man's trade and the requirements for the guilds were very high. Boys had to serve under an apprenticeship for six years—studying with a master knitter for three years and the other three years were met with traveling and learning techniques from knitters in other countries. Then, after that (as if that wasn't enough), they had to knit an intricate throw rug, a hat, a piece of clothing, and a pair of socks, all in a timely manner.

Women still cleaned and spun the wool for the men and now did some at-home knitting. Knitting was thought of as a valuable homemaking accomplishment and some brides even listed the skill as part of their dowry. However, women were not allowed to join the guilds unless a widow of a master knitter could demonstrate that she had also mastered the art of knitting.

Knitting came to the United States with the colonists. Its uses were purely practical as women and children, the primary knitters now, had little or no time for embellishment.

In the 19th century, the Industrial Age, the hand-knit industry was on a fast decline as knitting machines were invented and used for mass production of knitted fabric and articles of clothing.

In Great Britain in the late 1800s, knitting classes were required for students to prevent a complete loss of the art.

We seem to have finally come full circle and are experiencing a huge revival of the craft. Knitting today among girls and boys, women and men, is a testament to the long-standing honor and pride in the craft.

KNITTING BASICS

Although the projects in *The Portable Crafter: Knitting* were selected so that you can work on them while you are on the go, there are some knitting basics that should be considered before you step out of the door.

There is a depth and aliveness in natural fibers that you don't usually see in synthetics; however, they

have their place. For example, if the item is going to be used and laundered often, it may be more beneficial to use acrylic or other synthetic yarns.

Also, manufacturers have come out with some fabulous novelty yarns that can be used here and there for a splash of exciting embellishment to give the sweater, shawl, purse, hat, etc., more pizzazz. You will see several examples in the following pages of how these fun yarns can be used. Do not be afraid to experiment with them—the worst that can happen is you don't like it and take it out.

That being said, I love the texture and sensual feel of natural-fiber yarns: wool, cotton, silk, mohair, angora, alpaca, llama, and cashmere.

Alpaca feels as soft as cashmere and is a lot less expensive. Llama can be soft or scratchy depending on the grade. Merino wool is also extremely soft. Mohair is the fleece taken from an Angora goat. Cashmere is the fine downy wool at the roots of Kashmir goats. Finally, angora comes from Angora rabbits.

Cotton, as well, comes in different grades; pima, Egyptian, and green (no chemical added). The longer the cotton is on the plant, the softer it will be when spun, as there is less stubble when you spin a longer fluff of cotton (3"–4" versus 2"). Cotton yarn will stretch unless it has some other fiber with it. I like to use a brand that has 80% pima cotton and 20% merino wool. It is soft and does not stretch as easily.

SELECTING YARN WEIGHT

Yarn weight refers to the thickness of the strand of yarn. This thickness largely determines its gauge or how many stitches it will take to make up an inch of knitting.

For example, a medium-weight yarn may have a gauge of five stitches and seven rows to the inch, resulting in 35 stitches to the square inch. However, a heavy- or bulky-weight yarn, when worked on the same size needles, may only work up three stitches and five rows to the inch, resulting in 15 stitches to the square inch.

While there are no standardized categories for yarn weights, there are generalized terms that describe yarns by thickness and size of needle they are usually worked on. The label on the yarn will have this information:

Yarn	Needles	Stitches
Baby/fingering	1–3	7–8
Sport/baby	3–6	5–6
Chunky	5–7	5–5½
Worsted	7–9	4–5
Bulky	10–11	3–3½

CHECKING GAUGE

Your pattern will include a gauge notation (the number of stitches per inch) for the weight of yarn and size of needles required to make the sample. You may use the gauge provided as a guide, but the most reliable thing to do is to knit your own "gauge swatch" with the yarn you have chosen before starting any project. This way you can see if your tension equals the gauge called for in the pattern.

It is recommended that you knit a swatch in the pattern or stitches indicated that is approximately 4"–5" square. Press the finished square under a damp cloth and allow it to dry. Mark out the stitches indicated for gauge with blocking pins and measure the inches with your ruler or tape measure. (See Fig. 1 below)

If you have too many stitches per inch, you are working too tightly. You need to stitch with less tension or switch to larger needles. Similarly, if you have too few stitches per inch, you are working too loosely. In this case, you need

to stitch with greater tension or switch to smaller needles. Always remember to check your gauge.

ORGANIZING MATERIALS

Because you will be moving your knitting from place to place, you need a way to organize and carry all of your "stuff." Look for a bag that is large enough to hold your project, pattern, materials, and equipment. (See Fig. 2 below and Fig. 3 page 11) A bag with various-sized pockets is nice to have. Canvas or fabric totes work well as do small backpacks.

Fig. 2 - Organizing Materials

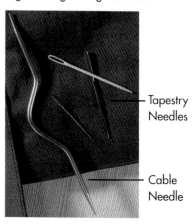

Tapestry Needles

Cable Needle

Fig. 1 - Checking Gauge

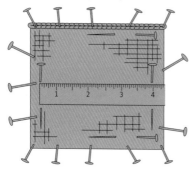

Fig. 3 - Organizing Materials

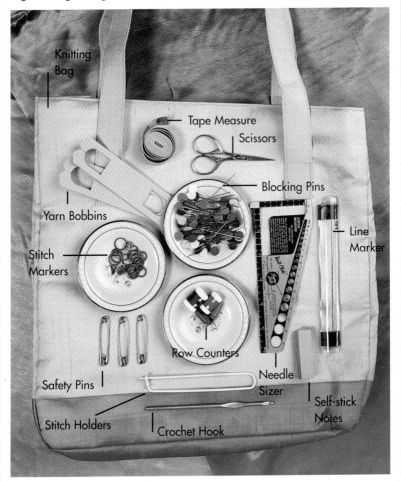

Knitting Bag

Tape Measure

Scissors

Blocking Pins

Yarn Bobbins

Line Marker

Stitch Markers

Row Counters

Safety Pins

Needle Sizer

Self-stick Notes

Stitch Holders

Crochet Hook

Knitting patterns are written in the language of knitting. These abbreviations are used for many of the repetitive words commonly found in knitting instructions.

BO = bind off

CC = contrasting color

c9f = cable 9 front—slip the next 5 stitches onto double-point needles and hold in front of work, knit next 4 stitches from left-hand needle, then knit stitches from double-point needle

CO = cast on

dec = decrease(ing)

dpn = double-point needle

garter st = knit each row, unless on a circular needle where you knit 1 round, purl 1 round

inc = increase(ing)—done usually by knitting in the front of a stitch and then knitting in the back before transferring it to the right-hand needle

k = knit

k2tog = knit 2 stitches together—a form of decrease

m1 = make 1 stitch

mb = make bobble—knit into front and back of stitch three times, making 6 stitches from 1. Lift second stitch on the right-hand needle over the first and off. Lift each stitch this way until there is just 1 remaining from the 6.

MC = main color

p = purl

p2tog = purl 2 stitches together—a form of decrease

Pick up = knit or purl into the loops or stitches along an edge

psso = slip 1 stitch into right-hand needle, knit the next stitch and pass the slipped stitch over the knitted stitch—a form of decrease

rep = repeat

rnd = round

RS = right side

seed st = knit 1, purl 1, knit 1 on odd number of stitches

sl	=	slip
ssk	=	slip, slip, knit—slip the next 2 stitches knitwise, 1 at a time onto the right-hand needle, then insert the tip of the left-hand needle into the fronts of these 2 stitches and knit them together—a form of decrease
st(s)	=	stitch(es)
St st	=	stockinette stitch—knit right side rows and purl wrong side rows
tog	=	together
WS	=	wrong side
yo	=	yarn over
*	=	are used before and after a group of stitches or steps to be repeated
( )	=	are used to indicate sts that are to be repeated the number of times specified. Example: *K1, (yo, k2) twice.* You would work k1, yo, k2, yo, k2.

Before beginning your project, it is a good idea to read through the entire pattern. It will give you an idea of how the item is structured and you will be able to visualize what the project will look like, and why and how it will look that way just by reading the pattern.

To help you along, there are instructions and diagrams for only a few techniques on pages 14–19. However, most of the stitches used in *Travel Knitting* are easily recognized by a seasoned knitter and are, therefore, not included.

If you come upon a stitch, pattern, or technique with which you are unfamiliar, there are several encyclopedias of knitting available in bookstores, knitting shops, and libraries that can help you. You can also go to your local knitting shop where there is bound to be someone who is willing to teach you how to accomplish the stitch.

WORKING WITH CHARTS

Charts are used in projects as shortcuts for explaining the color changes required in the pattern. Chartss are read right to left, bottom to top, and each square represents one stitch.

CROCHETING A CHAIN

Make a slip knot on the crochet hook as you would to cast onto a knitting needle.

1. Holding the hook like a pencil in your right hand and the yarn between the thumb and middle finger of your left hand, wrap the yarn up and over the hook (from back to front). (See Fig. 3)

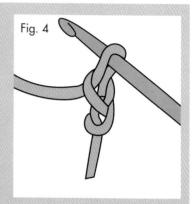

Fig. 4

Fig. 3

3. Repeat to desired length. (See Fig. 5) Cut yarn and pull through the loop.

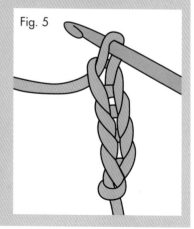

Fig. 5

2. Using hook, pull the yarn through the loop already on the hook. (See Fig. 4)

M1 (MAKE 1)

Make 1 results in an increase as you create a new stitch from the horizontal running thread between two existing stitches on the needle.

1. To make an increase that twists to the right on the RS, insert the tip of the left-hand needle under the running thread from back to front. (See Fig. 6)

Fig. 6

2. Knit into the strand as if it were a stitch. (See Fig. 7)

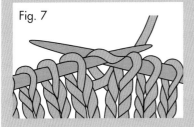

Fig. 7

3. To make an increase that twists to the left on the RS side, insert the tip of the left-hand needle under the running thread from front to back. (See Fig. 8)

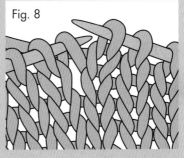

Fig. 8

4. Knit into the strand through the back of the loop as if it were a stitch. (See Fig. 9)

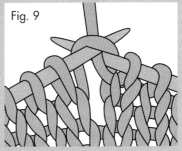

Fig. 9

PSSO (PASS SLIPPED STITCH OVER)
1. Slip the first stitch knitwise onto the right-hand needle. (See Fig. 10)

2. Once you have completed this action, knit the next stitch and pass the slipped stitch over it. (See Fig. 11)

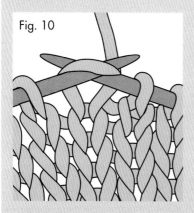

Fig. 10

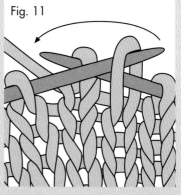

Fig. 11

Note: This stitch creates a single decrease that slants to the left. It is often paired with k2tog.

Note: If you discover an error in your work, correct it as soon as possible. If the error is a dropped stitch and is only one or two rows below the current one, you can retrieve it with your needles and continue without it being too noticible. If the error is a mistake in the pattern or a dropped stitch far below the current row, you must take the work off the needles and carefully pull the thread to the point of the error. Hold the yarn to the back when replacing needles and insert the tip into the front of the first stitch below the unpicked row.

PUTTING BEADS ONTO PERLE COTTON

1. Break one end of one strand of beads from your hank and tie a large knot in it. Break the other end of the strand from the hank so that it is free.

2. Fold the free end of the thread over onto itself forming a loop. Make an overhand knot to hold this loop in place. (See Fig. 12) If there is not enough thread exposed to make the knot, remove a few beads until there is enough room. You will have made the bead strand into a "string needle" having an eye at one end.

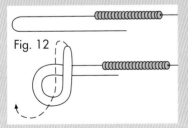

Fig. 12

3. Thread the loose end of your perle cotton through the eye of

your "string needle," leaving a tail of at least 8". (See Fig. 13)

Fig. 13

4. Carefully slide the beads over the knot and onto the perle cotton. If a bead refuses to slide over onto the perle cotton, unthread your string needle, remove the bead, and start the process again.

Notes: It is not essential to transfer all of the beads to the perle cotton before beginnng to knit. In doing a small amount at a time, the perle cotton gets less wear from the process of sliding the beads along it.

When you have knitted in all of the beads that you transferred onto the perle cotton, complete the row that you are working on, break the thread, and add more beads. Avoid trying to add beads in the middle of a row.

17

SEED ST (SEED STITCH)

1. On every other row, beginning with a RS row, knit one stitch, then purl one stitch, making certain to pass yarn between—not over—needles, to end of row.

2. On every other row, beginning with a WS row, purl one stitch, then knit one stitch to end of row.

3. Continue to alternate rows of stitches until knitted piece measures as indicated. (See Fig. 14)

Fig. 14

SL (SLIP)

Insert the right-hand needle tip purlwise into the first stitch on the left-hand needle and slip it off the left-hand needle onto the right-hand needle without knitting it or changing its orientation. (See Fig. 15)

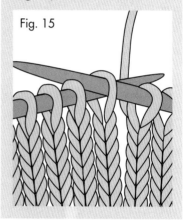

Fig. 15

Note: After binding off, secure the yarn end by threading it onto a tapestry needle and weaving it 2"–3" into the seam edge.

SHORT ROWS

Short rows create a tapered outside edge on the knitted piece that cannot be accomplished by decreasing methods.

In short rows, you do not knit to the end of the row. Instead, you knit part of the row, stop, and turn the work. Then you knit back again.

Short rows, if done incorrectly, can create holes in your work. To knit short rows without holes, you must take care to wrap a stitch at the turning point and knit the wrapped stitch on the next row.

1. Work short rows thusly:Knit as indicated to the turning point.

2. With the yarn at the back of the work, slip the next stitch onto the right-hand needle.

3. Pull the yarn forward between the needles.

4. Place the slipped stitch back onto the left-hand needle.

5. Pull the yarn back between the needles to the back of the work. This movement of the yarn creates a wrap around the base of the slipped stitch.

6. Turn the work. The yarn will be at the back of the work ready to purl on the next row.

7. Work to the wrapped stitch.

8. Insert the right-hand needle into the wrap and the stitch. Knit the wrap and the stitch together. (See Fig. 16)

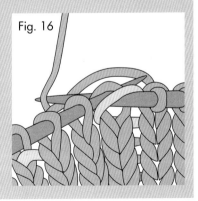

Fig. 16

19

FAST FLUFFY HAT

NEEDED ITEMS

- Yarn
    Bulky mohair and wool for the cream hat (200 yds) OR
    Caprice novelty big bumpy for the gray hat (200 yds)
- Needles
    circular, size 10.5
    double point, size 10.5
- Stitch markers

GAUGE
5 sts = 2"

INSTRUCTIONS

CO 60 sts on circular needle, being careful to not twist sts.

Work garter st in the round (k one row, p one row) until hat measures 8"–9", depending on how big a roll you want. End with a p rnd.

Using dpn:
Rnd 1—(K4, k2tog, place marker) 10 times.
Rnd 2 and all even rnds through rnd 6—P.

Rnds 3 and 5—(K to 2 sts before marker, k2tog) 10 times.
Rnd 7—K2tog around.

Break yarn, draw through remaining sts, and secure.

Weave in ends and tail.

> *Note: At first glance these hats may look frumpy and uninteresting. However, when you put one on it becomes something quite different. It can change with your whim—different colors, different yarns.*

POPPY HAT

NEEDED ITEMS

• Yarn

Brown Sheep Lambs Pride: MC (1 skein); CC1 (1 skein);
CC2 and CC3 (scrap lengths)

Worsted weight for hem (1 skein)

• Needles

circular, size 9 for small or size 10 for large

circular, size 7

double point, size 9 or 10

• Tapestry needle

GAUGE

on size 9 needles: 4 sts = 1"

on size 10 needles: 3.5 sts = 1"

INSTRUCTIONS

Using MC and CC1 tog, make a slip knot (this knot will be dropped and not counted as a stitch).

CO 80 sts using a long tail cast on. The CC1 will go over your thumb, the MC over your index finger, making the CC1 the edge.

After dropping the slip knot, join sts in the round. Place marker to indicate beginning of round.

K 2 rnds of MC.

Drop MC and join CC1. K 2 rnds and then start pattern (See Poppy Hat Chart on page 25), working from right to left, bottom to top and alternating CC1 and CC2.

When you have the desired length (6"–8"), shape top with MC:

22

Rnd 1—*K2tog, k2*, rep around. (60 sts)
Rnd 2—*K2tog, k8*, rep around.
Rnd 3—*K2tog, k7*, rep around.

Continue dec, working 1 less st between decs until 12 sts remain. K2tog around.

Break yarn, draw through sts, and secure. Weave in ends and tail.

HEM
With worsted weight and size 7 needles, pick up 1 st for every MC purl bump on inside of cast-on edge.Work in St st until ear lining is same width as pattern in hat. BO loosely.

EMBELLISHMENT
Make French knots for center of flower with CC3: Insert tapestry needle from WS of hat through middle flower. Wrap yarn around needle three times and insert needle in hat next to where it started. Gently pull needle through to WS of hat and secure. (See Fig. 17)

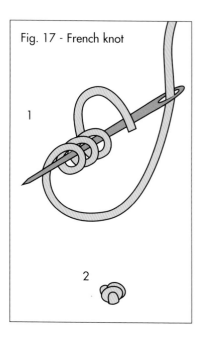

Fig. 17 - French knot

1

2

FINISHING
Loosely sew ear lining onto hat after weaving in all ends.

If desired, make tassel for top of hat and secure. (See Fig. 18)

Block hat over a head-sized bowl.

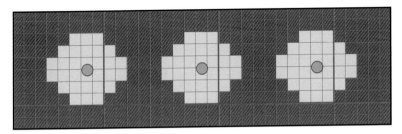

■ = CC1

□ = CC2

● = CC3

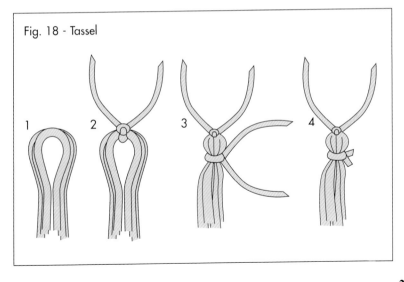

Fig. 18 - Tassel

1   2   3   4

BABY'S FIRST HAT

NEEDED ITEMS
• Yarn
  Brown Sheep Cotton Fleece or any worsted weight to give
    gauge: MC (100 yds); CC1 (10 yds); CC2 (10 yds)
• Needles
  circular, size 6
  double point, size 6

GAUGE
5 sts = 1"

SIZES
Sm will fit 0–9 mos. Med (in
parentheses) will fit 9–18 mos.

INSTRUCTIONS
CO 80 (88) sts.

Join tog being careful not to
twist and work St st in the round
(k every rnd) for 3½" (4½")
in MC.

Join CC1 and k 2 rnds, k 2 rnds
MC, k 2 rnds CC1, k 2 rnds MC,
k 2 rnds CC.

K 7 more rnds of MC and start
the dec:
K6, k2tog, rep to end of rnd.
K5, k2tog, rep to end of rnd.
K4, k2tog, rep to end of rnd.

Continue until you have 10 (11)
sts remaining. K these sts for 6
rows, then k2tog around.

Break yarn, draw through remaining sts, and secure.

Weave in ends and tail.

*Note: Pair hat with Striped
Baby Sweater on pages 82–84.*

For bells, buttons, or other embellishments, work St st in the round
for 4½" (5½"), p next rnd.

K 6 (7) more rnds and then start
dec as indicated. Sew embellishments onto decrease point.

FELTED PURSE

NEEDED ITEMS

- Yarn
    Galaway or any 100% wool, worsted weight (1 skein)
    Fizz (1 skein)
- Needles
    long double point, size 13
    straight, size 13
- Crochet hook, size 4
- Button

GAUGE

2.5 sts = 1"

SIZE

Approximate size before felting:
8" x 9"
Approximate size after felting:
6" x 7"

INSTRUCTIONS

Holding both yarns together, CO 44 sts on straight needle then take two dpn and hold them both in your right hand. Work from straight needle held in your left hand, knitting onto two dpn needles held in your right hand, k1 st on forward needle and k1 st on the back needle. Alternate sts in this manner until you have 22 sts on one needle and 22 sts on the other.

With the third dpn, garter st in the round (k1 row, p1 row—the first 2 rows are the most difficult). Continue working garter st in the round for 9".

BO 22 sts for the front.

ASYMMETRICAL FLAP

K1, k2tog, work to end of row. (Now you are knitting every row.) K one row plain.

29

Next row—K2tog, k to end.
Next row—K to last 2 sts, k2tog.
Continue dec every row in
this manner until you have
13 sts left.

Make buttonhole as follows:
K5 sts from the straight side of
flap. K2tog for buttonhole, k to
last 2 sts and k2tog. Next row still
dec, CO 1 st where you made the
buttonhole.

When you have 7 sts left on flap
and are on the straight side (not
angled), BO remaining sts. Draw
tail through last stitch. Weave
in ends.

SHOULDER STRAP
With two strands of worsted-wool
yarn held together, using crochet
hook, chain a rope about 60" long.
Pull tails through last st. Put this
"rope" in a mesh bag to felt in
washing machine.

FELTING
Place the articles to be felted in
the washing machine. Adding a
towel may help with the agitation
process.

Add a small amount of mild laun-
dry detergent and set temperature
to hot. The felting process usually
takes 12–18 minutes. For those
who have a top-loading machine,
you can check it (you should not
be able to see much, if any, light
through it when held up). Those
who have a front loading machine,
must wash for the longest amount
of time on the dial.

If the piece has not felted, repeat
the cycle. Take out, shape, and lay
flat to dry.

FINISHING
Before the purse dries, poke a
hole on each side of purse for
strap, and find the buttonhole.
(Insert a pen or pencil in these
holes to keep them open while
drying.) When dry, poke one end
of strap into one hole from the
inside and knot it. Repeat for the
other side; but before tying a knot,
put it on and measure for desired
length. Tie a knot and cut remaining length.

Sew on button.

FELTED CELL CASE

- Yarn
    Galaway or any 100% wool, worsted weight (1 skein)
    Mosaic (1 skein)
- Needles
    double point, size 13
    straight, size 13
- Button

GAUGE
2.5 sts = 1"

SIZE
Approximate size before felting:
5" x 7½"
Approximate size after felting:
3½" x 6½"

INSTRUCTIONS
Holding both yarns together,
CO 26 sts.

Refer to Felted Purse on pages
29–31. Divide as for purse so you
have 13 sts on each needle.

Work in garter st in the round
to 7"–7½".

BO 13 sts for front and continue
to work remaining 13 sts for flap.

Work for 2" in garter st.

Next row—K6, k2tog for buttonhole, k5.
Next row—K6, CO1, k6.

Work 4 more rows and BO.

FELTING
Refer to Felting on page 30. Felt
in washing machine.

FELTED COFFEE COZY

- Yarn
    mohair (1 skein)
    Nature Spun 100% wool, worsted weight (1 skein)
- Needles
    straight, size 13 or size to give gauge
- Crochet hook, size 1
- Button

GAUGE
2.5 sts = 1"

SIZE
Approximate size before felting:
13" x 5¾"
Approximate size after felting:
11" x 4¼"

INSTRUCTIONS
Holding both yarns together, CO 39 sts.

Work in garter st for 5¾" and BO.

Weave in ends with crochet hook.

BUTTON LOOP
Chain 3"–4" and attach to center of one short end of work.

FELTING
Refer to Felting on page 30. Felt in washing machine.

FINISHING
Sew on button.

LACY RIBBED SCARF

NEEDED ITEMS
- Yarn
  Douceur et Soie baby mohair, 70%/silk, 30% (2 skeins)
- Needles
  straight, size 6

GAUGE
5 sts = 1"

SIZE
10¼" x 56"

INSTRUCTIONS
CO 53 sts.

Work 10 rows in garter st.

PATTERN
Row 1—K5, place marker, k3, *yo, k2tog, k4*, rep from * five more times, yo, k2tog, k2, place marker, k5.

Row 2—K to marker, p across, sl marker, k5.

Work these 2 rows until almost all yarn is used. Remember to save enough for finish.

FINISHING
Work 10 rows in garter st.

BO.

Weave in ends and block.

CHUNKY SLIPPERS

NEEDED ITEMS
• Yarn
   Noro Multi OR Brown Sheep Lambs Pride [1 skein (125 yds)]
• Needles
   straight, size 9 or size to give gauge

GAUGE
3.5 sts = 1"

SIZES
Sm with cuffs (Med with cuffs
and Lg without cuffs)

INSTRUCTIONS
CO 21 (23, 27) sts. Work in seed
st (*k1, p1*, end k1) until piece
measures 1½" (1¾", 2") shorter
than foot.

Now work ribbing (k1, p1),
inc 1 st in last st on first row
of ribbing. Rib until slipper is
the length of foot.

Next row—(all sizes) K2tog
across row.

Adult sizes only can p one row,
k2tog across next row.

Cut yarn, leaving a tail that is
12"–15" long.

CUFFS
CO 10 (14, 14) extra sts. Work as
above until a little more than half
desired length. BO 5 (7, 7) sts of
the next 2 rows. Continue working
on remaining sts as above.

Thread tail on tapestry needle and pull yarn through remaining toe sts to close together.

Fold slipper and sew to instep or cuff. Weave in end.

Thread yarn from CO and sew heel seam.

Weave in ends.

OPTIONAL EMBELLISHMENTS

For the small-sized slippers, attach a decorative bead or bauble onto each. Those shown were cut from the ends of ponytail holders and sewn onto the slippers.

For medium-sized slippers, cut 1 yd of ¼" ribbon. Make a knot in the ribbon every 2"–3". With the yarn doubled on the needle, make a stitch between the knots.

When you have reached the end of the ribbon, place the thumb and forefinger of your left hand on the end of the ribbon.

Pull the end of the thread where needle is until ribbon pulls up into a little flower.

Secure and tie ribbon flower onto slipper with yarn so you can easily take the flower off when washing slippers.

For the large-sized slippers, embellish with covered buttons or any buttons. Those shown were covered with satin.

Note: My grandmother used to make these slippers for the whole family. She always made us feel special by individualizing them different embellishments—embroidery, tassels, buttons, etc. We mostly wore them at the cabin. The nights were cold and so were the beds. Gram would put large rocks in the oven of the wood-burning stove. When we were ready to go to bed, she would take a hot rock, wrap it in newspaper, and slip each rock between the sheets in our beds. Together with the slippers, our feet stayed warm and cozy.

HORSESHOE TOWEL

- Yarn
  Brown Sheep Cotton Fleece (1 skein)
- Needles
  straight, size 6
- Tapestry needle
- Stitch markers (optional)

GAUGE
5 sts = 1"

INSTRUCTIONS
CO 47 sts.

K3, place marker, k to last 3 sts, place marker, k3.

Work total of 4 rows in garter st.

PATTERN
Row 1—K3, sl marker, k1, *yo, k3, sl 1, k2tog, psso, k3, yo, k1*, rep from * to marker, k3.

Row 2 and all even rows—K3, sl marker, p to marker, sl marker, k3.

Row 3—K3, sl marker, k2, yo, k2, sl 1, k2tog, psso, k2, *yo, k3, yo, k2, sl 1, k2tog, psso, k2*, rep from * to last 5 sts, yo, k2, sl marker, k3.

Row 5—K3, sl marker, k2tog, (yo, k1) twice, *sl 1, k2tog, psso, (k1, yo) twice, sl 1, k2tog, psso, (yo, k1) twice*. Rep from * to last 10 sts, sl 1, k2tog, psso, (k1, yo) twice, sl 1, k1, psso, sl marker, k3.

Row 6—K3, sl marker, p to marker, sl marker, k.

Rep these 6 rows until towel is the desired length.

CO 8 sts.

Row 1—(RS) Sl 1, k2, yo, k2tog, (yo) twice (to make 2 sts), k2tog, k1. (9 sts)
Row 2—(WS) K3, p1, k2, yo, k2tog, k1.
Row 3—Sl 1, k2, yo, k2tog, k1, (yo) twice, k2tog, k1. (10 sts)
Row 4—K3, p1, k3, yo, k2tog, k1.

Row 5—Sl 1, k2, yo, k2tog, k2 (yo) twice, k2tog, k1. (11 sts)
Row 6—K3, p1, k4, yo, k2tog, k1.
Row 7—Sl 1, k2, yo, k2tog, k6.
Row 8—BO 3 sts (first st on right-hand needle), k4, yo, k2tog, k1. (8 sts)

Rep these 8 rows until edging is exactly the same width as your towel.

Using the tapestry needle, sew butterfly edging onto towel.

Weave in ends and block.

Notes: This is a small project that you can do on your lunch hour, in the car, plane, or train (my favorite way to travel.) I like to make up several in different colors and patterns to have on hand. On their own or wrapped around a lovely bar of soap, they make a great gift that can be used and appreciated.

If you want your towel to have a "vintage" look, give it a "tea bath" until the right "aging" is accomplished.

BASKET WEAVE TOWEL

NEEDED ITEMS

- Yarn
  Brown Sheep Cotton Fleece (1 skein)
- Needles
  straight, size 6
- Tapestry needle
- Stitch markers (optional)

GAUGE
5 sts = 1"

INSTRUCTIONS
CO 49 sts.

K3, place marker, k to last 3 sts, place marker, k3.

Work a total of 4 rows in garter st.

PATTERN
Row 1—K to marker, k3, *p7,k3*, rep from *, end k3, sl marker, k3.
Row 2—K to marker, p3, *k7, p3* rep from *, sl marker, k3.
Row 3—Rep Row 1.
Row 4—K3, sl marker, p43, sl marker, k3.
Row 5—K3, sl marker, p5, *k3, p7*, rep from *, end k3, p5, sl marker, k3.
Row 6—K3, sl marker, k5, *p3, k7*, rep from *, end p3, k5, sl marker, k3.
Row 7—Rep Row 5.
Row 8—Rep Row 4.

Rep these 8 rows until towel is desired length.

K 4 rows in garter st and BO.

CO 4 sts.

Row 1—Sl 1, yo, k1, yo, k2.
Row 2—Sl 1, k5.
Row 3—Sl 1, k1, yo, k2tog, yo, k2.
Row 4—Sl 1, k6.
Row 5—Sl 1, k2, yo, k2tog, yo, k2.
Row 6—BO 4 sts, k to end of row.

Rep these 6 rows until edging is the same width as your towel.

FINISHING
Using the tapestry needle, sew lace edging onto towel.

Weave in ends and block.

Basket weave close-up

BOBBLE CABLE TOWEL

NEEDED ITEMS
- Yarn
    Brown Sheep Cotton Fleece: MC (1 skein); CC (15 yds)
- Needles
    straight, size 6
    double point, size 6
- Tapestry needle
- Stitch markers

GAUGE
5 sts = 1"

INSTRUCTIONS
CO 49 sts.

K3, place marker, k to last 3 sts, place marker, k3.

Work total of 4 rows in garter st.

PATTERN
Row 1—K3, sl marker, seed st 7, place marker, p5, k9, p5, place marker, seed st 17, sl marker, k3.
Row 2 and all even rows—K3, sl marker, seed st 7, sl marker, k5, p9, k5, sl marker, seed st 17, sl marker, k3.

Rep Rows 1 and 2 once more.

Row 5—K3, sl marker, seed st 7, sl marker, p5, c9f, p5, sl marker, seed st 17, sl marker, k3.
Row 7—K3, sl marker, seed st 7, sl marker, p5, k4, join CC (k1, yf,

k1, yf, k1) into next st, turn and k5, turn and p5, turn and sl 1, k1, psso, k1, k2tog, turn and p3tog (one bobble completed), k4, p5, sl marker, seed st 17, sl marker, k3.
Row 8—Rep Row 2.

Rep Rows 1 and 2 twice more.

Rep these 12 rows until you have 16 bobbles.

Work 1 more cable row and then work 2 more rows.

Work 4 rows in garter st and BO.

BOBBLE LACE EDGE
CO 6 sts.

Row 1—Sl 1, k2, yo, k2tog, k1.

Row 2—Sl 1, k2, yo, k2tog, k1.
Row 3—Sl 1, k2, yo, k2tog, k1.
Row 4—K into the front and back of first st three times, making 6 sts from 1. Lift the second st on the right-hand needle over and off. The new second st is lifted over and off. Rep in this manner until only 1 st remains on the right-hand needle, k2, yo, k2tog, k1.

Rep these 4 rows until piece is the same width as your towel.

FINISHING
Using the tapestry needle, sew lace edging onto towel.

Weave in ends and block.

Note: The patterns for the body of each of the three towels shown on pages 42–50 would be perfect for making multiple panels that could be sewn together to make one large afghan. Try making the panels with worsted-weight yarn for a warmer knit. Make them with a single color of yarn so the patterns stand out or use several different colors of yarn for a more casual look. When the panels are pieced together, measure the width of one short edge of the afghan and make one of the lace edgings to equal that measurement. Sew the edging onto the afghan.

BEADED BAG

NEEDED ITEMS

- Perle cotton thread
  #8, pink [1 ball (10 grams)]
- Needles
  double point, size 0000
- Chain, silver, 2½'
- Purse frame, silver, 2⅜"
- Seed beads, size 11, purple iris (1 hank)
- Split rings, 6mm (2)

Designed by Theresa Williams

SIZE

2½" x 3¼"

INSTRUCTIONS

The front/back section of this project is knitted in one piece, starting at the top and then working down the front, across the bottom and up over the back side. Each side section is made up of one gusset that is knitted separately and sewn onto the front/back section.

While there is no need to increase or decrease stitches for the body of the frame-style bag, you must size the width of the bag to fit the frame. If it is too small, your options are to:

- use the larger size #000 needle.

- use the larger size 10 beads.
- cast on and place an extra 1 or 2 stitches at each end of the knitting,
- or some combination of the above options.

PUTTING BEADS ONTO PERLE COTTON
Refer to Putting Beads onto Perle Cotton on page 17. Put a portion of the seed beads—three strands at a time—onto the ball of perle cotton prior to beginning the knitting.

BEADED BAG
CO 23 sts.

Work as follows:
Rows 1–2—K23.
Rows 3–4—K4, (sl 1 bead, k1) 16 times, k3.
Rows 5–6—K4, (sl 2 beads, k1, sl 1 bead, k1, sl 1 bead, k1) five times, sl 2 beads, k4.
Rows 7–12—K4, (sl 2 beads, k3) five times, sl 2 beads, k4.
Rows 13–16—Rep Rows 5–6 two times.
Rows 17–22—Rep Rows 7–12 one time.
Rows 23–26—Rep Rows 5–6 two times.

Rows 27–32—Rep Rows 7–12 one time.
Rows 33–36—K2, (sl 1 bead, k1) two times, (sl 2 beads, k1, sl 1 bead, k1, sl 1 bead, k1) six times, k1.
Rows 37–42—Rep Rows 7–12 one time.
Rows 43–46—Rep Rows 33–36 one time.
Rows 47–52—Rep Rows 7–12 one time.
Rows 53–56—Rep Rows 33–36 one time.
Rows 57–62—Rep Rows 7–12 one time.
Rows 63–66—Rep Rows 33–36 one time.
Row 67—K3, (sl 1 bead, k2) 10 times.
Rows 68–69—K2, (sl 1 bead, k2) nine times, sl 1 bead, k3.
Rows 70–71—Rep Row 67 two times.
Rows 72–73—Rep Rows 68–69 one time.
Rows 74–75—Rep Row 67 two times.
Rows 76–77—Rep Rows 68–69 one time.
Rows 78–79—Rep Row 67 two times.

Rows 80–81—Rep Rows 68–69 one time.

Rows 82–83—Rep Row 67 two times.

Rows 84–85—Rep Rows 68–69 one time.

Rows 86–87—Rep Row 67 two times.

Rows 88–89—Rep Rows 68–69 one time.

Rows 90–91—Rep Row 67 two times.

Rows 92–93—Rep Rows 68–69 one time.

Row 94—Rep Row 67 one time.

Rows 95–98—Rep Rows 33–36 one time.

Rows 99–104—Rep Rows 7–12 one time.

Rows 105–108—Rep Rows 33–36 one time.

Rows 109–114—Rep Rows 7–12 one time.

Rows 115–118—Rep Rows 33–36 one time.

Rows 119–124—Rep Rows 7–12 one time.

Rows 125–128—Rep Rows 33–36 one time.

Rows 129–134—Rep Rows 7–12 one time.

Rows 135–138—Rep Rows 5–6 two times.

Rows 139–144—Rep Rows 7–12 one time.

Rows 145–148—Rep Rows 5–6 two times.

Rows 149–154—Rep Rows 7–12 one time.

Rows 155–156—Rep Rows 5–6 one time.

Rows 157–158—Rep Rows 3–4 one time.

Rows 159–160—Rep Rows 1–2 one time.

BO all sts.

GUSSETS

CO 4 sts.

Work as follows:

Rows 1–4—K4.

Row 5—K1, k1, inc 1, k1, inc 1, k1.

Row 6—K6.

Rows 7–50—K2, (sl 1 bead, k1) two times.

Row 51—K6.

Row 52—K1, k2tog, k2tog, k1.

Row 53—K4.

Because thread is so small, you may wish to place a safety pin or row counter every 10 rows to keep track of your rows.

BO all sts.

Rep for second gusset.

To sew the gussets or side panels into the side seams, fold the bag in half with right sides together, bringing the first and last rows together. Line up one gusset (this may be a little tricky because the gussets are so tiny) against the sides and bottom of the bag. With a tapestry needle, sew the gussets into the sides and bottom of the bag. Repeat for remaining gusset.

Weave in all ends.

Turn the bag right side out.

Match the inside center of the frame with the right side center-top edge of the bag. Safety-pin the top edge of the bag to the frame at the center and at each side. With a tapestry needle and working from the center toward one side of the bag, sew the top edge of the bag onto the frame. Secure thread at the base of the frame near the hinge, make a few backstitches, and tie off. Repeat in a similar manner for each quarter of the top edge of the bag and frame, until the bag is completely sewn into the frame.

Use any stitch that gives you the look you want. You can sew the bag onto the frame in such a way that the holes of the frame are covered, or you can leave the holes exposed.

If necessary, block lower portion of the bag.

Attach rings and chain onto the purse handle.

VARIATION
In place of the chain, you could make and attach a beaded neck-lace to further dress up the bag.

55

PLACE MAT

NEEDED ITEMS

- Yarn
    Euroflax 100% linen for MC, [1 skein (325 yds)]
    Fizz for CC (1 skein)
- Needles
    straight, size 6
- Stitch markers (2)

GAUGE
5 sts = 1"

SIZE
11½" x 17"

INSTRUCTIONS
CO 58 sts.

Work in garter st for 4 rows as follows: place marker after first 4 sts, work to last 4 sts, place marker, k4.

Row 5—K to marker, *yo, yo, k1*, rep from * to marker, k4.

Row 6—K to marker, *p1, drop yo, yo*, rep from * to marker, k4.
Row 7—K.
Row 8—Drop MC and join CC, p across.
Row 9—K across with CC.
Row 10—Break off CC and p across with MC. Work, keeping border, until piece measures 15". Drop MC and join CC on k row and k across. P the p row.

Rep Row 5.
Rep Row 6.

Work 4 rows in garter st and BO.

SIMPLE ELEGANT SCARF

NEEDED ITEMS
- Yarn
  Mountain Colors [1 skein (225 yds)]
- Needles
  straight, size 9
- Crochet hook, size 1

Designed by Susan Ure

GAUGE
4 sts = 1"

SIZE
9" x 38" without fringe

INSTRUCTIONS
Cut 60 12"-long pieces and save for fringe.

CO 30 sts.

Work all rows in garter st until you have used up all but 1 yd of yarn and BO.

FRINGE
Poke crochet hook into first st on first row. Fold one 12" piece of yarn in half, grab with crochet hook and pull partway through st. Pull the two ends of yarn through the loop that was just created. Rep for each st on first row.

Rep for sts on last row.

CABIN PILLOW

NEEDED ITEMS

- Yarn
    - Encore for MC (1 skein)
    - Encore for CC (1 skein)
- Needles
    - straight, size 8
- Buttons, large (3)
- Pillow form, 12"

Designed by Renee Groves

GAUGE
4 sts = 1"

SIZE
13" square

INSTRUCTIONS
With MC, CO 60 sts.

PILLOW FRONT
Work in St st for 6½".

With MC, work 4 rows in St st. Drop MC and join CC, work 5 rows seed st.

Rep these 9 rows four more times, ending with seed st pattern.

PILLOW BACK
With MC, work in St st for 14".

FLAP
Break MC and join CC, work (k2, p2) ribbing for 6½". BO in pattern.

FINISHING
Weave in ends. Fold piece after last seed st pattern at the bottom and sew front and back together.

Insert pillow form, fold ribbed flap down, and sew on buttons.

AURA PURSE

NEEDED ITEMS
- Yarn
    Aura from Trendsetter (1 skein)
    Knitaly from Colorado (1 skein)
- Needles
    16" circular, size 10.5
- Button

Designed by Allison Barlow

GAUGE
3.5 sts = 1"

SIZE
11" x 10"

INSTRUCTIONS
Holding both yarns together,
CO 26 sts.

Work in garter st for 34 rows.
(17 ridges)

At the end of the last row, CO 50
more sts and join in the round.

K all rnds until your piece
measures 10".

BO all sts and sew up bottom.

FINISHING
Make a drawstring cord 36" long
by twisting two strands together.

Make a shoulder strap to length
desired by twisting four strands
together.

Weave drawstring cord around
front and back of purse. Tie
in front.

Poke a hole on both sides of
purse, push one end of the shoulder strap through, and secure with
a knot.

Sew button onto top of flap.

LACY BABY SHAWL

NEEDED ITEMS
- Yarn
  merino wool, [14 skeins (1 ounce)]
- Needles
  circular, size 8

GAUGE
6 sts = 1"

SIZE
30" x 48"

INSTRUCTIONS
CO 180 sts.

Work in garter st for 8 rows for border. On last row, k6, place marker, k to last 6 sts, place marker, k6.

PATTERN

Row 1—K6, sl marker, k2tog four times, *(yo, p1) eight times, k2tog eight times*, rep from * across row ending with (yo, p1) eight times, k2tog four times, sl marker, k6.
Row 2—K across.
Row 3—K6, sl marker, p to marker, k6.
Row 4—K across.

Rep these 4 rows five more times, work 4 rows more in St st, keeping borders of garter (7 rows St st between sixth and seventh ridge), then rep from Row 1 until piece measures 48".

Work in garter st for 8 rows and BO.

WARM WRAP-UPS

Project 18

NEEDED ITEMS

- Yarn
    - Galaway worsted weight, charcoal for MC (3 skeins)
    - Galaway worsted weight, red for CC (1 skein)
- Needles
    - straight, size 10.5 or size to give gauge
- Buttons (2)
- Stitch markers

GAUGE

4 sts = 1"

SIZE

17½" x 52"

INSTRUCTIONS

With CC, CO 4 sts for pocket flap.

Row 1—K1, inc 1 in the next st, inc 1 in next st, k1. (6 sts)

Row 2 and all even rows—K across.

Row 3—K1, inc 1 in next st, k to 2 sts from the end, inc 1 in next st, K1.

Continue inc 2 sts every other row until you have 30 sts for the pocket flap. Join MC and break off CC. Work in garter st for 11".

SHAWL BODY

Row 1—(WS) K to end of row, then CO 8 sts.

Row 2—K across.

Row 3—K to end, CO 8 more sts.

Row 4—K across.

Row 5—K to end, CO 8 more sts. (54 sts)

Row 6—K to end, place marker, CO 11 sts for lace.

Row 7—K across.

Row 8—K54, k1, (yo, k2tog) four times, k2.

Row 9 and all odd number of rows through Row 23—K1, inc1, k to end of row.

Row 10—K54, k2, (yo, k2tog) four times, k2.

Row 12—K54, k3, (yo, k2tog) four times, k2.

Row 14—K54, k4, (yo, k2tog) four times, k2.

Row 16—K54, k5, (yo, k2tog) four times, k2.

Row 18—K54, k6, (yo, k2tog) four times, k2.

Row 20—K54, k7, (yo, k2tog) four times, k2.

Row 22—K54, k8, (yo, k2tog) four times, k2.

Row 24—K54, k9, (yo, k2tog) four times, k2.

Row 25—BO 8 sts loosely and k across.

Rep from Row 9 until you have 13 lace points. End with Row 25, k to end of row.

Next row—K across.
Next row—BO 11 sts, k across.
Next row—K across.
Next row—BO 8 sts, k across.
Next row—K across.
Next row—BO 8 sts, k across.
Next row—K across.
Next row—BO 8 sts, k across. (30 sts)

Work in garter st for 11".

Join CC and break off MC on RS, k across.

Next row—K1, k2tog, k to last 3 sts, sl 1, k1, psso, k1.
Next row—K across.

Rep the dec pattern until 4 sts remain. K last 4 sts and BO.

Weave in ends, fold pockets on RS, and sew up sides.

Sew a button onto each pocket flap.

Block.

BASIC SOCKS

Project 19

NEEDED ITEMS

- Yarn
    Brown Sheep Wild Foot or any sock yarn to give the
    gauge [1 (2, 2) skein(s)]
- Needles
    double point, size 2 or 3 or size to give gauge

GAUGE

15 sts = 2"

SIZES

Sm (Med and Lg). Size may need adjustment depending on length of foot.

LEG/ANKLE

CO 48 (56, 64) sts and divide evenly onto three needles. Work (k1, p1) ribbing for 4" (7", 8") or desired length to heel.

HEEL

Place 24 (28, 32) sts on one needle for heel, and remaining sts onto another needle to be used for instep. Adjust the sts to center the back above the heel. Work back and forth on the heel sts, starting with the RS, *sl 1, k1*, rep from *. Turn work, sl 1, p remaining sts on the next row.

Rep these 2 rows nine (11, 13) more times. Now you have 20 (24, 28) total heel rows. End ready to start a RS row.

TURN HEEL

Work to middle of row. K2, sl 1, k1, psso, k1, turn work.
Next row—Sl 1, p5, p2tog, p1, turn work.
Next row—Sl 1, k to 1 st from gap, sl 1, k1, psso, k1, turn work.
Next row—Sl 1, p to 1 st from gap, p2tog, p1, turn work.

69

Continue in this manner until all sts have been used from both sides. K to middle of the RS row.

With a free needle, k the second half of the heel sts. With the same needle, pick up 10 (12, 14) sts down left side of heel. Work across instep sts. With another free needle, pick up and k10 (12, 14) sts from right side of heel and work across remaining heel sts. Now you should have half of the heel sts, plus the picked up sts of left side on needle #1, the instep sts on #2 needle, the picked up sts on the right side, and the other half of the heel sts on #3 needle.

K to 3 sts from end of needle #1, k2tog, k1. Work across instep sts. At the beginning of the #3 needle, k1, ssk, k to end.
Next rnd—Work in St st.

Rep these 2 rnds, dec at the end of the #1 needle and at the beginning of #3 needle until you have a total of 48 (56, 64) sts.

Continue in St st on these sts until

70

the foot measures 1½" (2", 2¼") less than desired length from heel to toe.

Next rnd—Work to 3 sts from end of needle #1, k2tog, k1.

At the beginning of the instep sts on needle #2, k1, ssk, work to 3 sts from end of instep sts, k2tog, k1.

At the beginning of needle #3 k1, ssk and work to end.
Next rnd—work plain.

Rep these 2 rnds until you have 24 (28, 32) sts. Now work dec rnd as before only on every rnd until 8 sts remain.

Cut yarn, leaving a tail of 6"–8". Draw tail through remaining sts and pull snuggly. Weave in end on inside of sock and secure.

Make a tiny cable every fifth rnd by holding the yarn forward in your left-hand thumb and forefinger in the first k st (just after 2 purls), k the next st from left-hand needle, then k the st you are holding.

CHEVRON SCARF

NEEDED ITEMS
- Yarn
    Inca Alpaca [2 skeins (50 grams each)]
- Needles
    straight, size 6
- Stitch markers

GAUGE
11 sts = 2"

SIZE
6½" x 42"

INSTRUCTIONS
CO 37 sts.

Work in garter st for 6 rows.

PATTERN
Row 1—K5, place marker, * k1, yo, k4, k2tog, sl 1, k1, psso, k4, yo *, rep from *, end k1, place marker, k5.

Row 2—K5, sl marker, p27, sl marker, k5.

Rep these 2 rows until piece measures 42".

Work in garter st for 6 rows, starting on p side (WS) row. BO on WS.

Weave in ends and block.

CHEVRON HAT

NEEDED ITEMS
- Yarn
  - Inca Alpaca [1 skein (50 grams)]
- Needles
  - circular, size 6
  - double point, size 6
- Tapestry needle

GAUGE
11 sts = 2"

SIZE
Sm

INSTRUCTIONS
CO 104 sts onto circular needle.

Join in the round and place marker. Work (k2, p2) ribbing for 6 rows.

K for 2 rounds.

PATTERN
Row 1—*K1, yo, k4, k2tog, sl 1, k1, psso, k4, yo*, rep from * seven more times to end of row. Sl marker.
Row 2—K.

Rep these 2 rows 14 more times or to desired length. K 2 rnds.

DECREASE
Row 1—*K6, k2tog*, rep from * to end.
Row 2 and all even rows—K.
Row 3—K5, k2tog, rep to end.
Row 5—K4, k2tog, rep to end.
Row 7—K3, k2tog, rep to end.
Row 9—K2, k2tog, rep to end.
Row 11—K1, k2tog, rep to end.
Row 13—K2tog across.

Thread tail onto tapestry needle and run it through the 13 remaining sts, pull tightly and fasten off.

Weave in ends on inside and block.

BASIC BABY SWEATER

NEEDED ITEMS
- Yarn
    worsted weight [1 skein (3½ ounces)]
- Needles
    straight, size 6
    circular, size 8
    double point or cable, size 6
- Crochet hook, size 1
- Stitch holders
- Stitch markers

Designed by Beth Epperson

GAUGE
on size 8 needle: 4 sts = 1"

SIZE
6 mos.

INSTRUCTIONS
Wind off small ball for sleeve and front.

CO 49 sts onto smaller-sized straight needles.

Row 1—(WS) Work ribbing (p1, k1) to end of row. Work this rib pattern for neck for 5 rows total.
Row 6—(RS) Change to circular needle, rib 4 (k1, p1, k1, p1), k7, place marker, k4, place marker, k19, place marker, k4, place marker, k7, rib 4. These markers delineate the fronts, sleeves, and back.
Row 7 and all WS rows—Work ribbing (p1, k1) on edges, p body and sleeves.
Row 8—(RS) Work ribbing (k1, p1) k to 1 st before first st of each

marker, inc 1 st before and 1 st after markers. (57 sts now on needle).

Inc 12 more rows as above. (13 total increases, 153 sts total)

(WS) Work across left front and put those sts on a holder, work across left sleeve, work across back, and put the back on a holder. Work across right sleeve and put the sts of the right front on a holder. At this point, you will be working on the sleeves.

(RS) Work first sleeve (left). Join small ball of yarn to the right sleeve and work across. Work 2" on sleeves then start dec on each side of sleeves thusly: K1, k2tog, k across to last 3 sts, sl 1, k1, psso, k1. Work 2" more and dec again as before. For ribbed cuff, k sleeves to 6½", then work garter st for 5 rows and BO. Sew up the completed sleeves.

FRONT AND BACK (FROM HOLDER)
Pick up left front that has not been worked and join ball of yarn, p across, keeping the 4 sts in ribbing.

(RS) Work left front, pick up 1 st in sleeve, work across back, pick up 1 st in sleeve, work right front. (95 sts) Work body of sweater until length measures 6½", work 5 rows in garter st and BO.

FINISHING
Weave in ends. With crochet hook, on bottom of right side, work single crochet to neck. For left side, work from neck down.

A single buttonhole is made by pushing the button through an opening in the sts.

> *Note: This baby sweater and the three that follow on pages 79–87 are all made from the same basic pattern. The simple variations and the yarn that was selected to work them up makes them different. You will likely want to knit each one.*

SEED BABY SWEATER

NEEDED ITEMS

- Yarn
    worsted weight [1 skein (3½ ounces)]
- Needles
    straight, size 6
    circular, size 8
    double point or cable, size 6
- Crochet hook, size 1
- Stitch holders
- Stitch markers

Designed by Beth Epperson

GAUGE
on size 8 needle: 4 sts = 1"

SIZE
6 mos.

INSTRUCTIONS
Wind off small ball for sleeve and front.

CO 49 sts onto smaller-sized straight needles.

Row 1—(WS) Work seed st to end of row. Work this pattern for neck for 5 rows total.

Row 6—(RS) Change to circular needle, seed st 4, k7, place marker, k4, place marker, k19, place marker, k4, place marker, k7, seed st 4. These markers delineate the fronts, sleeves, and back.

Row 7 and all WS rows—Work seed st on edges, p body and sleeves.

Row 8—(RS) Work ribbing (k1, p1) to 1 st before first st of each marker, inc 1 st before and 1 st after markers. (57 sts now on needle)

Start seed st pattern on first inc row (Row 8), working 2 rows seed st, then 2 rows plain, then 2 rows seed st. (Remember on all even rows to inc before and after each marker—13 total incs, 153 sts total.)

(WS) Work across left front and put those sts on a holder, work across left sleeve, work across back, and put the back on a holder. Work across right sleeve and put the sts of the right front on a holder. At this point, you will be working on the sleeves.

(RS) Work first sleeve (left). Join small ball of yarn to the right sleeve and work across. Work 2"

on sleeves then start dec on each side of sleeves thusly: K1, k2tog, k across to last 3 sts, sl 1, k1, psso, k1. Work 2" more and dec again as before. For cuff, k sleeves to 6½", then seed st for 5 rows and BO. Sew completed sleeves.

FRONT AND BACK (FROM HOLDER)
Pick up left front that has not been worked and join ball of yarn, p across, keeping the 4 sts in seed st.

(RS) Work left front, pick up 1 st in sleeve, work across back, pick up 1 st in sleeve, work right front. (95 sts)

Work body of sweater until length measures 6½", work seed st for 5 rows and BO.

FINISHING
Weave in ends.

A single buttonhole is made by pushing the button through an opening in the sts.

STRIPED BABY SWEATER

NEEDED ITEMS

- Yarn
    Brown Sheep Cotton Fleece: MC [1 skein (3½ ounces)]; CC (10 yds)
- Needles
    straight, size 5
    circular, size 7
    double point or cable, size 6
- Crochet hook, size 1
- Stitch holders
- Stitch markers

Designed by Beth Epperson

GAUGE

on size 7 needle: 5 sts = 1"

SIZE

0–3 mos.

INSTRUCTIONS

Wind off small ball for sleeve and front.

CO 49 sts onto smaller-sized straight needles.

Row 1—(WS) Work ribbing (p1, k1) to end of row. Work this rib pattern for neck for 5 rows total.

Row 6—(RS) Change to circular needle, rib 4 (k1, p1, k1, p1), k7, place marker, k4, place marker, k19, place marker, k4, place marker, k7, rib 4. These markers delineate the fronts, sleeves, and back.

Row 7 and all WS rows—Work ribbing on edges, p body and sleeves.

Row 8—(RS) Join CC and work ribbing to 1 st before first marker, inc 1 st before and after each marker, inc 8 sts (57 sts now on needle). Rep for another row. Join

MC and rep for 2 rows, then join CC and rep for 2 more rows. Join MC and rep for 7 more rows. (13 total incs, 153 sts total)

(WS) Work across left front and put those sts on a holder, work across left sleeve, work across back, and put the back on a holder. Work across right sleeve and put the sts of the right front on a holder. At this point, you will be working on the sleeves.

(RS) Work first sleeve (left). Join small ball of yarn to the right sleeve and work across. Work 2" on sleeves then start dec on each side of sleeves thusly: K1, k2tog, k across to last 3 sts, sl 1, k1, psso, k1. Work 2" more and dec again as before. For rolled cuff, k sleeves to 7" and BO. Sew up the completed sleeves.

FRONT AND BACK (FROM HOLDER)
Pick up left front that has not been worked and join ball of yarn, p across, keeping the 4 sts in ribbing.

(RS) Work left front, pick up 1 st in sleeve, work across back, pick

up 1 st in sleeve, work right front. (95 sts)

Work body of sweater until length equals the length of the sleeves for a rolled edge and BO.

FINISHING
Weave in ends. With crochet hook, on bottom of right side, work single crochet to neck. For left side, work from neck down. Chain 1 for buttons if desired.

A single buttonhole is made by pushing the button through an opening in the sts.

CABLE BABY SWEATER

NEEDED ITEMS
- Yarn
  Brown Sheep Cotton Fleece [1 skein (3½ ounces)]
- Needles
  straight, size 5
  circular, size 7
  double point or cable, size 6
- Crochet hook, size 1
- Stitch holders
- Stitch markers

GAUGE
on size 7 needle: 5 sts = 1"

SIZE
0–3 mos.

INSTRUCTIONS
Wind off small ball for sleeve and front.

CO 49 sts onto smaller-sized straight needles.

Row 1—(WS) Work ribbing (p1, k1) to end of row. Work this rib pattern for neck for 5 rows total.

Row 6—(RS) Change to circular needle, rib 4 (k1, p1, k1, p1), k7, place marker, k4, place marker, k19, place marker, k4, place marker, k7, rib 4. These markers delineate the fronts, sleeves, and back.

Row 7 and all WS rows—Work ribbing on edges, p body and sleeves.

Row 8—(RS) Work ribbing to 1 st before first marker, inc 1 st before and after each marker, inc 8 sts

85

(57 sts now on needle), inc 12 more rows as above. (13 total incs, 153 sts total)

(WS) Work across left front and put those sts on a holder, work across left sleeve, work across back, and put the back on a holder. Work across right sleeve and put the sts of the right front on a holder. At this point, you will be working on the sleeves.

(RS) After first inc on left sleeve, p1, put 3 sts on cable needle and hold in front. K3 from left needle, then k3 from cable needle, p1, inc 1 in next st as indicated in pattern. K across back, working incs at marker. After working first inc on right sleeve, p1, put 3 sts on cable needle and hold in front. K3 from left needle, k3 from cable needle, p1, inc in next st as indicated in pattern.

(WS) Rib, p to marker, p2, k1, p6, k1, p2, p across back to marker, p2, k1, p6, k1, p2, p to ribbing.

Work in established pattern of inc and cable every sixth row, keeping with incs, and then decs.

For rolled cuff, work sleeves to 6" then work in St st for 1" and BO.

Pick up left front that has not been worked and join ball of yarn, p across, keeping the 4 sts in ribbing.

(RS) Work left front, pick up 1 st in sleeve, work across back, pick up 1 st in sleeve, work right front. (95 sts) Work body of sweater until length equals the length of the sleeves for a rolled edge and BO.

Weave in ends. With crochet hook, on bottom of right side, work single crochet to neck. For left side, work from neck down. Chain 1 for buttons if desired.

A single buttonhole is made by pushing the button through an opening in the sts.

MITTENS & SCARF

NEEDED ITEMS
• Yarn
   double-knitting chenille (4 skeins)
• Needles
   straight: size 6, size 4, size 3
   double point, size 6
• Tapestry needle

Designed by Penny Toliver

GAUGE
on size 6 needles: 5 sts = 1"

SIZES
Scarf is 11" x 58". Mittens are Med, or 4" x 9½". If necessary, adjust needle size to obtain the correct gauge.

INSTRUCTIONS
Note: Refer to the following list of abbreviated terms for working with cable needles (you may wish to photocopy this list to have on hand while knitting):

T5R	Sl 3 sts onto cable needle and hold at back of work, k2, then p1 from cable needle.
T3B	Sl 1 st onto cable needle and hold at back of work, k2, then p1 from cable needle.
T3F	Sl 2 sts onto cable needle and hold at front of work, p1, then k2 from cable needle.
C3R	Sl 2 sts onto cable needle and hold at front of work, k1, k2 from cable needle.

C3L   Sl 1 st onto cable needle and hold at back of work, k2, then k1 from cable needle.

C6   Sl 3 sts onto cable needle and hold at back of work, k3, then k3 from cable needle.

SCARF

With size 6 needles, CO 67 sts.

Rows 1, 3, 5, 7—K.
Rows 2 and 6—P1, *k1, p1*, rep from * to end of row.
Rows 4 and 8—K1, *p1, k1*, rep from * to end of row.

CABLE PATTERN

Row 1—(K1, p1) twice, p1, k6, p1, k43, p1, k6, p1, (p1, k1) twice.
Row 2—(K1, p1) twice, k1, p6, k1, p43, k1, p6, k1, (p1, k1) twice.
Row 3—(K1, p1) twice, p1, C6, p1, k43, p1, C6, p1, (p1, k1) twice.
Row 4—Rep Row 2.
Rows 5–10—Rep Rows 1–2 three times.
Row 11—(K1, p1) twice, p1, C6, p1, k19, T5R, k19, p1, C6, p1,

(p1, k1) twice.
Row 12—(K1, p1) twice, k1, p6, k1, p21, k1, p21, k1, (p1, k1) twice.
Row 13—(K1, p1) twice, p1, k6, p1, k18, T3B, k1, T3F, k18, p1, k6, p1, (p1, k1) twice.
Row 14—(K1, p1) twice, k1, p6, k1, p20, k1, p1, k1, p20, k1, p6, k1, (p1, k1) twice.
Row 15—(K1, p1) twice, p1, k6, p1, k17, T3B, k1, p1, k1, T3F, k17, p1, k6, p1, (p1, k1) twice.
Row 16—(K1, p1) twice, k1, p6, k1, p19, (k1, p1) twice, k1, p19, k1, p6, k1, (p1, k1) twice.
Row 17—(K1, p1) twice, p1, k6, p1, k16, T3B, (k1, p1) twice, k1, T3F, k16, p1, k6, p1, (p1, k1) twice.
Row 18—(K1, p1) twice, k1, p6, k1, p18, (k1, p1) three times, k1, p18, k1, p6, k1, (p1, k1) twice.
Row 19—(K1, p1) twice, p1, C6, p1, k15, T3B, (k1, p1) three times, k1, T3F, k15, p1, C6, p1, (p1, k1) twice.
Row 20—(K1, p1) twice, k1, p6, k1, p17, (k1, p1) four times, k1, p17, k1, p6, k1, (p1, k1) twice.
Row 21—(K1, p1) twice, p1, k6, p1, k14, T3B, (k1, p1) four times,

k1, T3F, k14, p1, k6, p1, (p1, k1) twice.

Row 22—(K1, p1) twice, k1, p6, k1, p16, (k1, p1) five times, k1, p16, k1, p6, k1, (p1, k1) twice.

Row 23—(K1, p1) twice, p1, k6, p1, k14, C3R, (p1, k1) four times, p1, C3L, k14, p1, k6, p1, (p1, k1) twice.

Row 24—Rep Row 20.

Row 25—(K1, p1) twice, p1, k6, p1, k15, C3R, (p1, k1) three times, p1, C3L, k15, p1, k6, p1, (p1, k1) twice.

Row 26—Rep Row 18.

Row 27—(K1, p1) twice, p1, C6, p1, k16, C3R, (p1, k1) twice, p1, C3L, k16, p1, C6, p1, (p1, k1) twice.

Row 28—Rep Row 16.

Row 29—(K1, p1) twice, p1, k6, p1, k17, C3R, p1, k1, p1, C3L, k17, p1, k6, p1, (p1, k1) twice.

Row 30—(K1, p1) twice, k1, p6, k1, p20, k1, p1, k1, p20, k1, p6, k1, (p1, k1) twice.

Row 31—(K1, p1) twice, p1, k6, p1, k18, C3R, p1, C3L, k18, p1, k6, p1, (p1, k1) twice.

Row 32—(K1, p1) twice, k1, p6, k1, p21, k1, p21, k1, p6, k1, (p1, k1) twice.

Row 33—(K1, p1) twice, p1, k6, p1, k19, T5R, k19, p1, k6, p1, (p1, k1) twice.

Row 34—(K1, p1) twice, k1, p6, k1, p43, k1, p6, k1, (p1, k1) twice.

Rep Rows 3–34, to desired length from 48" to 58" and ending with Row 34.

Rep Rows 3–8 once.

(RS) Rep first 8 rows worked before cable pattern.

BO all sts.

FINISHING
Block.

Cut four 13" pieces of yarn. Fold all pieces in half as one.

(WS) Poke crochet hook from front to back through scarf at one corner of one short edge. Catch pieces of yarn at fold and pull through to front of scarf, creating a loop. Pull yarn ends through loop. Pull yarn ends taut. Rep across edge of scarf.

Rep for remaining short edge of scarf.

MITTENS
With size 3 needles, CO 43 sts.

LEFT-HAND MITTEN
Work ribbing thusly:
Row 1—K1, *p1, k1*, rep from * to end of row.
Row 2—P1, *k1, p1*, rep from * to end of row.

Rep these 2 rows until piece measures 2" and ending with RS row.

Inc row as follows: P1, *k1, p1*, rep from * to end of row, inc 1 at end of row (44 sts).

Change to size 4 needles. Work 6 rows in St st.

Next row—K19, m1, k2, m1, k to end of row.
Next row—P.
Next row—K19, m1, k4, m1, k to end of row.

Continue to m1 at each side of thumb gusset as before on second and every following alternating row to 54 sts and ending with a WS row.

SHAPE THUMB
Work in short rows thusly:
Next row—K32, turn.
Next row—P14, turn.

Working on these 15 sts only, work 12 rows.

Next row—(K2tog) seven times, k1.
Next row—P.
Next row—(K2tog) four times, k1.

Break yarn, leaving a 6" tail.

Thread tail onto tapestry needle and run it tightly through remaining sts on knitting needles. Remove knitting needles. Pull yarn tightly, and weave in end to close edge and form top of thumb.

MITTEN BODY
(RS) Join yarn to remaining sts, pick up and k2 sts from base of thumb, k to end of row. (43 sts)

Next row—P.
Work 24 rows.

SHAPE TOP
Work as thusly:
1st row—K2tog, k18, sl 1, k2tog, psso, k to last 2 sts, k2tog.
2nd row and every following alternating row—P.
3rd row—K2tog, k16, sl 1, k2tog, psso, k to last 2 sts, k2tog.
5th row—K2tog, k14, sl 1, k2tog, psso, k to last 2 sts, k2tog.
7th row—K2tog, k12, sl 1, k2tog, psso, k to last 2 sts, k2tog.
9th row—K2tog, k10, sl 1, k2tog, psso, k to last 2 sts, k2tog.
10th row—P. (23 sts)

BO all sts.

RIGHT-HAND MITTEN
Rep from CO to change to size 4 needles and work 6 rows St st for left-hand mitten.

Work thusly:
Next row—K22, m1, k2, m1, k to end of row.
Next row—P.

Next row—K22, m1, k4, m1, k to end of row.

Continue to m1 at each side of thumb gusset as before on 2nd and every following alternating row to 54 sts and ending with a WS row.

SHAPE THUMB
Work in short rows thusly:
Next row—K35, turn.
Next row—P14, turn.

Working on these 15 sts only, work 12 rows.

Next row—(K2tog) seven times, k1.
Next row—P.
Next row—(K2tog) four times, k1.

Rep from break yarn to BO all sts for left-hand mitten.

FINISHING
Block each mitten.

Sew all seams.

Weave in all ends.

Leanne Bennett's first knitting project was in the second grade when her mother taught her how to knit diaper covers for her teacher's new baby. Since then, she has knit everything from suits to socks, taught family and friends how to knit, has had a small knitting business, and has sold her hand-knits at various venues from craft fairs to ski lodges.

Now she prefers small portable projects like hats, gloves, scarves, and socks because they work up fast and she can take them anyplace. Besides knitting, Leanne practices Yoga and sells real estate in Salt Lake City, Utah, where she resides. In the summer, she offers weekend knitting retreats in her 100-year-old cabin.

If you have questions or comments, or would like more information, Leanne can be contacted at 801-581-0234 or via e-mail at knitsandstitches@hotmail.com.

CONVERSION CHART

inches to millimetres and centimetres
(mm-millimetres, cm-centimetres)

inches	mm	cm	inches	cm	inches	cm
⅛	3	0.3	11	27.9	31	78.7
¼	6	0.6	12	30.5	32	81.3
⅜	10	1.0	13	33.0	33	83.8
½	13	1.3	14	35.6	34	86.4
⅝	16	1.6	15	38.1	35	88.9
¾	19	1.9	16	40.6	36	91.4
⅞	22	2.2	17	43.2	37	94.0
1	25	2.5	18	45.7	38	96.5
1¼	32	3.2	19	48.3	39	99.1
1½	38	3.8	20	50.8	40	101.6
1¾	44	4.4	21	53.3	41	104.1
2	51	5.1	22	55.9	42	106.7
3	76	7.6	23	58.4	43	109.2
4	102	10.2	24	61.0	44	111.8
5	127	12.7	25	63.5	45	114.3
6		15.2	26	66.0	46	116.8
7		17.8	27	68.6	47	119.4
8		20.3	28	71.1	48	121.9
9		22.9	29	73.7	49	124.5
10		25.4	30	76.2	50	127.0

INDEX